BLAKE'S JERUSALEM

THE STORY OF THE W.I. SONG

ERNIE RICHARDS

BLAKE'S JERUSALEM

THE STORY OF THE WI SONG

WORDS: WILLIAM BLAKE
1757 – 1827
MUSIC: SIR HUBERT PARRY
1848 – 1918

For years now, people have talked about the WI as 'they're all about Jam and Jerusalem'. That is, they are always making jam and they are always singing 'Jerusalem'.

Despite all the new activities and new Institutes, despite the Calendar Girls raising millions for cancer research, that is still the image of the WI to the general public. So what's wrong with jam making and singing 'Jerusalem'?

The jam represents not only a little sweetness in life, but also all the nourishment that WIs have always been involved with. Two World Wars – and the WI was started in the middle of the first one, remember - and two home fronts, with women not only making munitions and all the other jobs left to do when the men went off to fight, but also responsible for keeping the nation fed. They were the land girls working all over the country. 'Dig for Victory' was the slogan: gardens were turned into allotments, women learnt how to grow and cook fruit and vegetables to feed their families and the nation.

This has always been the driving force of the WI.

So jam represents all the cooking and nurturing that women do for their families and neighbours.

So what about 'Jerusalem'.

Why are they always singing this?

Why not 'Land of Hope and Glory' or 'Rule Britannia' or even 'I vow to thee my country'? They are all stirring patriotic songs to inspire a nation.

What has 'Jerusalem' got to do with the members of WIs?

Everything – they were there at the start: not of the words which William Blake wrote over 200 years ago, but at the rebirth of the words in 1915 and at the birth of the music written in 1916.

THE MUSIC
SIR HUBERT PARRY 1848 – 1918

1915 was a key year in the story. In 1915, the very first WI in Great Britain was started in Anglesey in the village of LlanfairPG and they then spread rapidly all over the country. Two Institutes claimed to be the first in England, Singleton in West Sussex and Wallisdown in Dorset, both started in Autumn 1915. The National Federation was formed in 1917 - there were by then 187 Institutes, with a total membership of over 5,000.

In 1915, the Poet Laureate, Robert Bridges, produced an anthology called 'The Spirit of Man'. This was designed to raise the morale of the nation, severely depressed by a year of harsh war and thousands of casualties. Blake's poem, neglected for over 100 years, appealed to Bridges enormously and he included it in his anthology.

He found the poem an excellent text to inspire hope in the middle of death and destruction and he asked the well-known composer Sir Hubert Parry to put it to music for a Fight for Right Campaign meeting in London's Queen's Hall.

The aims of this organisation were 'to brace the spirit of the nation, that the people of Great Britain, knowing that they are fighting for the best interests of humanity, may refuse any temptation, however insidious, to conclude a premature peace, and may accept with cheerfulness all the sacrifices necessary to bring the war to a satisfactory conclusion.'

Bridges asked Parry to supply 'suitable, simple music to Blake's stanzas – music that an audience could take up and join in.' And that is exactly what Parry did.

The piece was to be conducted by Parry's former student, Walford Davies, but Parry was reluctant to set the words, because he had doubts about the ultra – patriotism of the Fight for Right movement.

Not wanting to disappoint either Robert Bridges or Walford Davies he agreed, writing it on 10th March 1916 and giving it to Davies with the comment 'Here's a tune for you old chap: do what you like with it.'

Davies later recalled:

'We looked at the manuscript together in his room at the Royal College of Music, and I recall vividly his unwonted happiness over it ...... He ceased to speak, and put his finger on the note D in the third stanza where the words 'O clouds unfold' break his rhythm. I do not think any word passed about it, yet he made it perfectly clear that this was the one note and one moment of the song which he treasured.'

Davies arranged for the vocal score to be published by Curwen in time for the concert at the Queen's Hall on 28th March 1916 and began rehearsing it.

It was a success, and soon was requested by a whole range of organisations, including the WI.

But Parry soon had serious misgivings about the Fight to Right movement, and withdrew his support in 1917. There was even a worry that he might also withdraw 'Jerusalem', but this situation was saved by Millicent Garrett Fawcett of the National Union of Women's Suffrage Societies (NUWSS). The song had been taken up by the Suffragettes in 1917 and Millicent Fawcett asked Parry if he would agree to the song being used at a Suffrage Demonstration Concert on 13th March 1918. Parry was delighted and orchestrated the piece for that occasion. (Originally it had only been scored for voices and organ, or piano.)

After the concert Millicent Fawcett wrote to Parry, saying

'Your Jerusalem ought to be made the women voters' hymn'

Parry replied,

'I wish indeed it might become the women voters' hymn, as you suggest. People seem to enjoy singing it. And having the vote ought to diffuse a great deal of joy, so they should combine happily.'

He then went on to give the copyright of the music to the NUWSS.

The links between the people who founded the WI and the suffragists are incredible strong. It is significant that both the first General Secretary – Inez Fergusson (later Jenkins), and the first Treasurer of the NFWI, Helena Auerbach, had previously worked for the NUWSS; indeed Helena had been Treasurer for them first. Grace Hadow who became Vice-Chairman of the NFWI had previously been involved with the Oxford Students' Branch of the NUWSS and had also set up a branch of the NUWSS in Cirencester.

For years, the WI organisation had been looking for a suitable hymn or song to sing at their monthly meetings and at their big gathering, the Annual General Meeting. Many songs were suggested, but nothing was thought suitable. A national competition was organised for people to write their own songs, with very mixed results!

Gertrude Lampson, of the East Sussex Federation, set the tone:

'It seems to me that a song which is intended to express the ideas and ideals of a body of people is a very important thing, and must have lasting quality about both words and music. It has to inspire not only one generation but also successive ones. A trivial tune, set to second-rate words, would soon be worn to a shred like a garment of inferior material. Now at the start of the Women's Institute movement, the National Federation was most fortunate in having the late Mr Willy Leslie, a very fine musical amateur, to guide them in their choice of song; and I think that, once the matter has been considered, you will agree that Jerusalem was a very wise decision.'

The decision to choose Jerusalem came as a result of a letter to Home and Country in the December prior to the 8th AGM, from Vice-Chairman Grace Hadow:

'I have recently been at Exhibitions or Council Meetings at which the whole assembly has joined in singing Sir Hubert Parry's setting of Blake's Jerusalem. Many WI members have said how much they would like to sing it at our Annual Meeting in London, and I write to urge that WIs or County Federations which approve of this suggestion might write to Headquarters and ask if this could be arranged.

'It should be clearly understood that when a WI makes this request, it pledges itself to learn words and tune by heart. The attempt cannot be a success unless every delegate is ready to sing whether she thinks she can sing or whether she thinks she cannot. Both words and music are simple and dignified and easy to learn. Incidentally the learning would give pleasure to any WI and would afford an excellent opportunity for a short talk either on Blake's poetry, or on poems about England. We have looked in vain for a national 'Institute Song'. Here is one made to our hand and one which some counties have already adopted.

Grace E Hadow'

Mr Willy Leslie of Llansantffraid persuaded Sir Walford Davies, a personal friend, to make a special arrangement for string orchestra for the AGM, while he himself conducted the singing, bringing a choir from local WIs with him to lead.

It was sung for the first time at the 8th Annual General Meeting held in the Queen's Hall, London on Tuesday 20th and Wednesday 21st May 1924. The Queen's Hall was almost entirely filled by the 2,300 delegates and visitors from all over the country.

From the April 1924 Home and Country:

'The year's annual meeting will have one special feature. The delegates will burst into song. It must be a great inspiring shout of song or the outside world will be in no way impressed. Jerusalem was a happy choice, for as the delegates sing hopefully of the New Jerusalem which every Institute member is helping to build, the singers can remember with thankfulness that 'satanic mills' no longer disgrace our lands. Blake's protest on behalf of the helpless child victims of those thoughtless days was not made in vain.'

When women got the vote, in 1928, the NUWSS was disbanded having achieved its aims. Parry's Executors gave the copyright to the WI, who kept it until it came out of copyright in 1968.

So, for 40 years, it was not only the song that the WI sang at all its meetings, but it was theirs legally and morally.

And they are still revelling in singing this stirring music.

Why 'Jerusalem' and not 'Land of Hope and Glory' or 'Rule Britannia'?

They are all wonderful, stirring tunes.

But only the poem 'Jerusalem' was written by a poetic genius.

The secret is in the words. The other patriotic anthems tend to glorify England and the British Empire and are complacent about Britain and her natural place in the world.

But Blake, while he celebrates England, questions conditions in this country, and wants his readers to take action.

The words carry the inspirational meaning. What do they really mean and who was William Blake?

THE WORDS
WILLIAM BLAKE 1757 – 1827

William Blake was born in London in 1757 and apart from a brief period of 3 years in the countryside at Felpham in Sussex he lived in London all his life, dying there in 1827.

Blake was a revolutionary in politics and in literature: an extraordinary man who lived life by his own standards and would never compromise. He was always poor, but never stopped working at what he wanted to do, and never gave up on his life's 'mission'. His ideas sprang out of his concern for the ordinary working people of London: their poverty, hunger, lack of education and poor health. He thought it was everyone's duty to try to improve conditions for everyone else.

This concern shines through most of his shorter poems and is seen in his life.

Blake taught himself about politics and literature. He learned to read and write in school, but for all the rest, like Jane Austen and the Bronte girls, he learnt by reading voraciously, anything and everything.

He was lucky to find a woman who shared his feelings, and shared in the daily work he did.

When he was 25 and staying in rented rooms in London, he fell hopelessly in love and asked the girl to marry him. She refused. He was broken-hearted and told the family he was visiting about his rejection.

The daughter of the house sympathised with him. 'I am very sorry for you,' she said.

'Are you really sorry for me?' asked Blake. 'Then I will love you.'

The girl called Catherine Boucher was bowled over by Blake. She experienced a 'peculiar nervous sensation which she could not explain or describe.' As soon as he came into the room Catherine had 'instantly recognised her future partner' and 'was so near fainting that she left his presence until she had recovered.'

After their first interview, he determined to marry her. He gave himself a year to earn enough money to provide for her and set up as an engraver.

When she had to sign the marriage register the girl had to put a cross, because she couldn't read or write.

'Don't worry,' said the bridegroom, 'I will teach you.'

And so he did. And not only that, but he taught her how to help him in his job, which was making engravings. She became very skilled at colouring in the engravings by hand. And so they lived and worked together very contentedly. Catherine was a stabilising influence on him and calmed him when he got angry as he did frequently.

That could be the story of almost any poor couple in the 18th or 19th century – except for one thing: not many bridegrooms could teach their bride to read and write – even if they could read and write themselves. And more importantly not many bridegrooms would think it worthwhile to teach their wife something as completely useless as reading and writing. Why teach women to read? They'd only waste their time reading trashy romances. (And so they did – but they could and did read other things as well, including Mary Woolstonecraft and Tom Paine and the Bible, Shakespeare, Milton....) Being able to read opens the door to all the thinkers, poets and novelists who have ever lived.

But this wasn't any ordinary poor man and wife. Blake believed in equality and if he found something which wasn't equal, he would change it if he could.

Blake was a man with a vision, and a plan: to wake up England to the inequalities in society, and to the cruelties the rich inflicted on the poor.

He was a revolutionary, but he was also a Christian – that is a follower of Jesus Christ. He had nothing to do with the vengeful God of the Old Testament, but everything to do with the good shepherd. He had nothing to do with the Church of England, or any established church. He had everything to do with living his own version of the Christian story:

'I must create a system or be enslaved by another man's ....

I will not reason and compare: my business is to create.'

And create his own system he did.

He was a mystic. From an early age and right through his life, he saw Angels who spoke to him.

Many people thought he was mad but Wordsworth said,

'There was no doubt this poor man was mad, but there is something in the madness of this man which interests me more than the sanity of Lord Byron and Walter Scott.'

A young man asked a friend of Blake:

'Do you not think he's cracked?'

'Yes, sir," replied the friend 'but his is a crack that lets in the light.'

His craft was engraving and he earned his living by making engravings for other people.

In his spare time he would do his own work – and this was something special. He literally produced his own books, printed, coloured and stitched together.

He wrote poems not on paper but on metal. He wrote directly onto a copper plate. Usually he did drawings to go with the poems. The poems had to be written backwards so that when the plate was printed, they would come out the right way. Then he printed them together on one page, as black and white reproductions. (For a very full description of the process see 'Blake' by Peter Ackroyd pages 112 to 114.)

Then he added colours, painting them on by hand, each page separately.

Soon, he would have enough to make a small book and he would stitch the pages together laboriously.

This process was time-consuming and tedious and there was a big problem with what he produced.

Nobody wanted them. No-one wanted to buy them and no-one wanted to read them. They didn't like the poems and they did not like his illustrations.

But nothing stopped him. He just kept on and on producing his illustrated poems which Catherine hand-coloured in. He could not afford to doubt his own abilities. He wrote,

'If the sun and moon should doubt

They'd immediately go out.'

Revolution was in the air – the revolt of the American Colonies and the French Revolution had encouraged a lot of people in England to agitate for reform of the social system in England, by taking power away from the rich, and giving it to all the people: the basic principle of democracy.

It is possible that he was a friend of Tom Paine, the corset-maker from Thetford in Norfolk, who, while helping to confine women's bodies, also helped to free their minds. He had encouraged through his writings, and physical presence, both the American War of Independence and the French Revolution. Blake certainly admired his books 'The Rights of Man' and 'Common Sense.' Paine had a price on his head for allegedly promoting 'treason' and, if he were caught in England, he would be put to death – and so would anyone who had been hiding him.

Blake is reputed to have hidden Paine in his house for several days and, if he did, they doubtless talked over the problems of the world. Not just in theory. Although they disagreed on many things, they were both of them visionaries, in that they knew what kind of life they wanted for everyone, but practical in that they suggested how these things could be done.

Blake knew Mary Woolstonecraft – the mother of the Mary who married Shelley and wrote 'Frankenstein'.

Mary Woolstonecraft was married to the philosopher William Godwin and wrote 'A Vindication of the Rights of Women' published amazingly in 1792 – one year after Paine's 'The Rights of Man'.

Questions of equality were being discussed passionately by various groups, and Blake was part of many of those groups.

He expressed his concerns in his first few poems.

The vast bulk of Blake's poetry is contained in a series of very long poems, on mythical or classical subjects. Blake uses a vocabulary and a system of symbols that constitutes a private language, making the poems very difficult to understand.

On the other hand, his shorter poems communicate with a directness that is invigorating and deeply moving.

He has an extraordinary ability to see into the heart of things:

'To see a World in a Grain of Sand
And a Heaven in a Wild Flower,
Hold Infinity in the palm of your hand
And Eternity in an hour.'

His first two books were called 'Songs of Innocence' completed in 1789, and 'Songs of Experience' completed in 1794.

In his lifetime, he produced only 24 copies of the complete series of poems!

In these poems, he is concerned about the plight of children: The Little Black Boy, The Chimney Sweeper, The Little Boy Lost, The Little Boy Found, Infant Joy, The Little Girl Lost, The Little Vagabond and The School Boy.

In some of these, he writes as though to a small child. In others, he writes as though he were a small child. In most of them, though the thoughts may be complex the expression is always as simple as he can make it.

Let us look at a few examples:

In 'The Lamb', we see a deceptive simplicity: Jesus as a lamb. He is capable of great tenderness as here, where he takes on the persona of a little child talking to a lamb.

The poem begins with:

> 'Little Lamb, who made thee
> Dost thou know who made thee?'

And the poem ends with these lines:

> Little Lamb, I'll tell thee,
> Little Lamb, I'll tell thee:
> He is called by thy name,
> For he calls himself a Lamb.
> He is meek, & he is mild;
> He became a little child,
> I, a child, & thou a lamb,
> We are called by his name.
>> Little Lamb, God bless thee!
>> Little Lamb, God bless thee!

Contrast this simplicity with the complex power of The Tiger, the poem that most of us read in school.

> Tiger, Tiger, burning bright,
> In the forests of the night;

What immortal hand or eye,
Could frame thy fearful symmetry?
In what distant deeps or skies
Burnt the fire of thine eyes!
On what wings dare he aspire?
What the hand, dare seize the fire?

And what shoulder, & what art,
Could twist the sinews of the heart?
And when thy heart began to beat,
What dread hand? & what dread feet?

What the hammer? What the chain,
In what furnace was thy brain?
What the anvil? What dread grasp,
Dare its deadly terrors clasp?

When the stars threw down their spears
And water'd heaven with their tears:
Did he smile his work to see?
Did he who made the Lamb make thee?

Tiger, Tiger burning bright,
In the forests of the night:
What immortal hand or eye,
Dare frame thy fearful symmetry?

Could the same divine force that produced the lamb also have produced the restless coiled energy that is the tiger?

In this poem, Blake taps in to the power and energy of the sun or of fire – both of which can make life and destroy life.

Tapping into this divine energy is to touch the source of life itself.

<u>He hates cruelty to any living thing</u>: birds, animals –

'A Robin Red breast in a Cage
Puts all Heaven in a Rage.
A dove house fill'd with doves & Pigeons

Shudders Hell thro' all its regions.
A dog starv'd at his Master's Gate
Predicts the ruin of the State.'

<u>Blake hated racial prejudice and slavery</u> and shows this in his poem 'The Little Black Boy'. This begins:

'My mother bore me in the southern wild,
And I am black, but O! my soul is white;
White as an angel is the English child,
But I am black, as if bereav'd of light.

And ends with these two verses:

'Thus did my mother say, and kissed me;
And thus I say to little English boy:
When I from black and he from white cloud free,
And round the tent of God like lambs we joy,

I'll shade him from the heat, till he can bear
To lean in joy upon our father's knee;
And then I'll stand and stroke his silver hair,
And be like him, and he will then love me.'

This theme is repeated in the 20th century in Martin Luther King's famous speech 'I have a dream', given in Washington, August 28th, 1963.
'.....I have a dream that one day this nation will rise up and live out the true meaning of its creed: 'We hold these truths to be self-evident; that all men are created equal.' ....
'I have a dream that my four little children will one day live in a nation where they will not be judged by the colour of their skin but by the content of their character......
'I have a dream that one day down in Alabama with its vicious racists, with its governor having his lips dripping with the words of interposition and nullification, one day right there in Alabama little black boys and little black girls will be able to join hands with little white boys and white girls as sisters and brothers.....'

He hates cruelty to women: marriage was often a prison for a wife, with her husband as a jailer, owning all of her possessions and owning her body and mind.

SONG
How sweet I roam'd from field to field,
And tasted all the summer's pride,
'Till I the prince of love beheld,
Who in the sunny beams did glide!

He shew'd me lilies for my hair,
And blushing roses for my brow;
He led me through his gardens fair,
Where all his golden pleasures grow.

With sweet May dews my wings were wet,
And Phoebus fir'd my vocal rage;
He caught me in his silken net,
And shut me in his golden cage.

He loves to sit and hear me sing,
Then, laughing, sports and plays with me;
Then stretches out my golden wing,
And mocks my loss of liberty.

This is a beautiful song of love and joy, but it ends in imprisonment. It may be a beautiful cage, but it is still a cage.

He hates cruelty to all the poor people living in London and throughout the whole country. 'The mind-forged manacles I hear' – the restrictions that stop the mind working out alternatives to the current enormities.

LONDON
I wander thro' each charter'd street,
Near where the charter'd Thames does flow,
And mark in every face I meet

Marks of weakness, marks of woe.

In every cry of every Man,
In every Infant's cry of fear,
In every voice, in every ban,
The mind-forg'd manacles I hear.

How the Chimney-sweeper's cry
Every black'ning Church appals;
And the hapless Soldier's sigh
Runs in blood down Palace walls.

But most thro' midnight streets I hear
How the youthful Harlot's curse
Blasts the new born Infant's tear,
And blights with plagues the Marriage hearse.

<u>*And where is love in all this?*</u>

Love starts with the family – husband and wife and their children and then moves out into the community: to the poor and sick and needy. The last two verses of 'William Bond' are:

'I thought Love lived in the hot sun shine,
But O, he lives in the Moony light!
I thought to find Love in the heat of day,
But sweet Love is the Comforter of Night.

Seek Love in the Pity of others' Woe,
In the gentle relief of another's care,
In the darkness of night & the winter's snow,
In the naked and outcast, Seek Love there!'

JERUSALEM

To look now at the actual poem which we know as 'Jerusalem'. This had no title and was set at the start of one of Blake's very long poems 'Milton'. When first printed, it looked like this:

MILTON
A POEM IN 2 BOOKS
To Justify the Ways of God to Men
Written and etched, 1804 – 1808
PREFACE

.... Rouze up, O Young Men of the New Age! Set your foreheads against the ignorant Hirelings! For we have Hirelings in the Camp, the Court and the University, who would, if they could, for ever depress the Mental and prolong corporeal War. Painters! On you I call. Sculptors! Architects! ……….. believe Christ and his Apostles that there is a Class of Men whose whole delight is in Destroying. We do not want either Greek or Roman Models if we are but just and true to our own Imaginations, those Worlds of Eternity in which we shall live for ever in JESUS OUR LORD.

    And did those feet in ancient time
    Walk upon England's mountains green?
    And was the holy Lamb of God
    On England's pleasant pastures seen?

    And did the Countenance Divine
    Shine forth upon those clouded hills?
    And was Jerusalem builded here
    Among these dark Satanic Mills?

    Bring me my Bow of burning gold:
    Bring me my Arrows of desire:
    Bring me my Spear: O clouds unfold!
    Bring me my Chariot of fire.

    I will not cease from Mental Fight
    Nor shall my Sword sleep in my hand
    Till we have built Jerusalem
    In England's green and pleasant Land.

    "Would to God that all the Lord's people were Prophets"
                  Number xi. ch., 29 v.

Why would Blake write a long poem about Milton?

Because he admired him above all other poets.

Milton, who lived from 1608 – 1674 in the thick of religious and civil wars, was the poet most admired by the poets of the 18th and 19th centuries. His was the voice of religion, of common sense, of justice and freedom. 'Paradise Lost' set out 'To Justify the Ways of God to Men.' As well as his poems, Milton wrote persuasively on subjects very much alive then and now. He wrote a huge defence of freedom for the press, called 'Areopagitica,' and although he was a devout Christian, he advocated freedom for married couples to divorce, if they could no longer live together amicably. He is the voice of passionate reason – the moral compass of the nation.

As a kind of preface to Milton, Blake wrote the poem 'And did those feet….'

Blake uses the same subtitle – 'to Justify the Ways of God to Men' – as Milton does in 'Paradise Lost'.

The prose preface: there is an earlier paragraph which I have left out, which is about the need of not copying from the past, but creating from within yourself.

This second paragraph is a call to action. Rouse up, young men of the new age. Defy those who would stop us thinking, and who would lead us into continual wars.

He calls on artists of all kinds to recognise that there are people whose main purpose in life is to destroy – people's hopes and ambitions and self-beliefs. We do not need to follow classic patterns: we must create our own works of art coming from our own imaginations.

The poem we now call 'Jerusalem' does not refer to the historical town in the Middle East. Nor does it mean the great long poem in four books that Blake wrote.

It was first known as:

'And did those feet in ancient time,'

And only changed when Parry made his orchestral version of the musical setting in 1918.

For Blake in this poem, Jerusalem stands for the home of peace, where Christ's law of love prevails, and where men and women live in fellowship together.

It is an ideal city, where ugly things like fear, greed, cruelty and injustice do not exist. The first two verses of 'Jerusalem' show us a dream, and the last two verses are a call to action.

In verses one and two, Blake uses a traditional legend, which is that Jesus could have visited England when he was between 12 and 30 years old, a period when the Gospels have nothing to say about him.

It is known that a trade in tin and lead went on in early times between England and the Phoenicians. There is a tradition that Joseph of Arimethea was involved in this trade: the idea occurs in a song used by the miners.

If, as many historians believe, Joseph of Arimethea was related to Mary, the mother of Jesus, it is possible that Jesus, as a young man, may have accompanied Joseph on some of his travels.

This tradition survives in Cornwall, at Glastonbury in Somerset and at Priddy on the Mendip Hills, where we know there was trade in lead around the time of Jesus.

Perhaps Blake heard of this story, when he visited Priddy. He would have found a small village in the centre of the ancient lead and copper mining area. The entrances to the disused mines still show, dark and terrible, against the green hillsides. The local people believed that these hills were always green because they were once trodden by the feet of Jesus.

What may also have given Blake the feeling of 'England's pleasant pastures' was his three year stay in the rural village of Felpham.

His return to London would have reminded him forcibly of the 'dark satanic mills.' At the end of the road where Blake lived stood the ruins of the new, highly-automated Albion Mill. This was the first great factory in London designed to run on steam-engines and to produce 6,000 bushels of flour a week. It was one of the 'sights' of London, but in March 1791, just after Blake moved into his house in Lambeth, it was burned down. Arson was strongly suspected. The factory was destroyed and remained as a black ruined shell until 1809 – Blake would pass it every time he walked into the city. But Blake knew that up and down the country hundreds of mills were working and employing women and children on long hours, with no protection from dangerous machinery, and earning a pittance – a form of slavery, which was accepted by society.

The 'dark satanic mills' is the turning point of the poem: the last line of verse two releases the anger that Blake feels about the treatment of God's creatures: treating human beings as worse than beasts of the field. His fury comes out as righteous anger, and he summons up all the armoury of God – of the Old and New Testaments – to combat the evils he sees around him.

Bring me my bow, my arrow and my spear – all very unfeminine things for women to wield. Blake explains more in a verse letter he wrote while at Felpham:

> 'With the Bows of my mind and the Arrows of thought,
> My bowstring fierce with ardour breathes,
> My arrows glow in the golden sheaves.'

Then let the clouds unfold as they did for Elijah, to bring him a chariot of fire – which will burn the evil away.

The power of thinking can outweigh physical prowess and when directed against the enemy – the people who exploit and enslave others, the people who would control our freedom to think for ourselves – it can destroy.

In the last verse he commits himself to a fight to build Jerusalem in 'England's green and pleasant land.'

The fight will not be easy, and it will not be won quickly. So he will not stop his mental fight, and the spear and the sword become his psychological weapons.

He commits himself in this poem – not us.
But the act of singing the words as a group does commit us – the 'I' becomes 'we'. The power of the words coupled with the drive of the music becomes a commitment.

At the end of the poem Blake adds a quotation from Numbers 11: 29
"Would to God that all the Lord's people were Prophets"

By prophets Blake does not mean people who prophesy or foresee the future. Christopher Rowland, Professor of Theology at Oxford University, argues that 'prophets includes everyone in the task of speaking out about what they saw. Prophecy for Blake, however, was not a prediction of the end of the world, but telling the truth as best a person can about what he or she sees, fortified by insight and an 'honest persuasion' that with personal struggle, things could be improved. A human being observes, is indignant and speaks out: it's a basic political maxim which is necessary for any age. Blake wanted to stir people from their intellectual slumbers, and the daily grind of their toil, to see that they were captivated in the grip of a culture which kept them thinking in ways which served the interests of the powerful.'

The words of the poem 'stress the importance of people taking responsibility for change and building a better society in England's green and pleasant land.'

So, that is the reason why WIs sing 'Jerusalem' rather than 'Rule Britannia' or 'Land of Hope and Glory.' They are committing to improving people's lives in whatever way they can.

Some people think that all the inequalities that Blake was concerned about have now been eradicated.

But Clare Short (Secretary of State for International Development from 1997 to 2003 in Tony Blair's government) said this:

'Women do most of the world's work, earn little of its income, own less of its wealth, are absent from forums of power, do most of the caring for the weak, and suffer too frequently from abuse. All over the world, women's demands for an equal chance in life is the most revolutionary political force there is.'

Clare Short is talking about women world-wide, but a glance at any daily paper will show how her comments are still true for this country.

In the words of Nelson Mandela: 'The impossible is only impossible until it is done.'

Gertrude Lampson has the last word:

'So when we sing this tremendous poem let us remember that Blake's vow to fight and to go on fighting evil and injustice should be our vow. The magic of both words and music is surely great enough to stir us into thought and action. Let us make the ideal of 'Jerusalem' not just a pious hope, but a reality in our own lives, in our homes and in our country.'

TRIBUTE

I would like to pay tribute to the women of the WI, throughout its near 100 years existence. First, to all those pioneers fighting initially for the right to vote, but then extending this to include making life worth living – the right to education, employment, health, equality before the law and in everyday life.

Their achievements have been extraordinary as a glance at the WI book entitled *Speaking Out* will show: the list of Resolutions passed at their AGM and subsequently acted upon.

But so much more remains to be done. I hope that the spirit of 'Jerusalem' will carry them forward to fresh achievements in their second century.

Acknowledgements

For help in compiling this booklet, my thanks are due first to my partner Aleathia Mann without whom there would have been no booklet, to Anne Stamper, archivist to the NFWI, for invaluable help with information, to 'Home and Country', the WI magazine (the forerunner of WI Life,) to the East Sussex Federation for a leaflet by an unnamed author, and to Gertrude Lampson, for an inspirational leaflet on the words and the music. Mrs Lampson was Chairman of the Music sub-committee of the East Sussex Federation of WIs from 1920 – 1957. (How about that for service?) She was obviously passionate about the benefits of choral singing, and about the need to know exactly what it is you are singing.

Any factual errors are mine, and of course all opinions expressed are mine.

Copyright 2014
Published and printed by Ernie Richards, Springwood, Church Lane, Sparham, Norwich NR9 5PP
Telephone 01362 688075

Ernie Richards was born in Liverpool and went to the Liverpool Institute High School (Paul McCartney's old school, which is now the Liverpool Institute for the Performing Arts.)

He read English at Cambridge University and for many years was head of the Arts Department at I.M. Marsh College in Liverpool (now part of the Liverpool John Moores University.)

He was recently Principal of Urchfont Manor College in Wiltshire.

His other booklets include:

Shakespeare's Women in Love – a look at how Shakespeare presents the women in his plays.

"He does what no other writer has done – or could do. He presents women as the one force in society capable of saving mankind from itself: the essential earth-mother, the nurturing force behind everything born, and the solver of problems. He shows that women can be the main force in society for civilising men, for curbing their instincts to fight and kill, and to replace those violent impulses with the gentler arts of tolerance, love and forgiveness.

"His position is not only that women are the equal of men, which would be a revolutionary belief in that age, as in most other periods before the twentieth century. But he shows that they are superior to men in certain definite aspects. A more challenging notion could not be imagined then – or even now. He demonstrates this superiority in most of his plays."

Coming soon to celebrate the Centenary of the Women's Institute - two booklets:

Makers of the Movement: Studies of six pioneers of the movement.

100 Things every Woman should know: essential facts and figures for the modern woman. Events that helped shape our world today.

Printed in Great Britain
by Amazon